WELCOME TO LONDON'S CHURCHES

An introduction to a variety of London's Churches

By PHIL MASON

© Phil Mason 1985.

Published by
NORHEIMSUND BOOKS AND CARDS
1 Whitney Road
Burton Latimer
Kettering
Northants NN15 5SL

INDEX

COVER PHOTOGRAPHS:

Top left—The City Temple
Top right—St. Marylebone
Bottom left—St. Martin in the Fields
(by courtesy of Frank Rust)
Bottom right—Westminster Cathedral

Every effort has been made to ensure that the details given are correct at the time of going to press. However the times of services may change (especially weekday services) and these should be checked by telephone.

ST. MARTIN-IN-THE-FIELDS
Trafalgar Square

This masterpiece by James Gibbs, a follower of Sir Christopher Wren, was consecrated in 1726. As well as being the Parish Church of the Sovereign (part of Buckingham Palace stands in the Parish) it could be called the Parish Church of the 'Londoner' and the Commonwealth, and is without doubt the best loved Parish Church in the Anglican Communion.

This is probably due to two reasons, the now famous overseas broadcasts which link the friendly church near Charing Cross to people the world over, and the social work for those in need.

Side by side with the routine parish work of services, clubs and meetings, is the caring, and St. Martin's cares in a big way. While visitors look around the church a steady stream of people make their way down the steps to the basement of the Vicarage where the Social Service unit is situated. They come, young and old, with problems ranging from a broken marriage, to drug addiction, the need of a bed for the night, or just sheer loneliness. No one is ever turned away. On Sundays a soup kitchen in the Crypt caters for up to 400 men who seek warmth and companionship.

In 1914 a new vicar named Dick Sheppard took the locks off the private pews, which were rented by the fashionable residents of Mayfair, and opened the door to all who wanted to enter. Those doors are still open with each subsequent vicar making a contribution and adapting the work to meet the needs of a changing world.

Seven hundred years ago a small Chapel stood in the fields half way between the Abbey of Westminster and the city of London. It was used by wayfarers, and the monks as they travelled from the Abbey to work in the Convent Garden (now Covent Garden). The Chapel was dedicated to St. Martin who shared his cloak with a beggar. A fitting dedication to a Church that shares the love of Jesus with the needy.
St. Martin's is not a museum but a workshop. A church that offers love, and in doing so has discovered that love still works miracles.

INFORMATION

SUNDAY SERVICES

8.00	Holy Communion (1662)
9.45	Family Communion
11.30	Morning Service
12.30	Holy Communion (first and third Sunday in month)
3.00	Service in Cantonese
4.15	Choral Evensong
6.30	Evening Service
7.30	Holy Communion (first Sunday in the month)

WEEKDAY SERVICES

8.00	Mattins
8.15	Holy Communion
5.30	Evensong (not Saturday)
6.00	Homegoing Prayers (not Thursday or Saturday)
1.05	WEDNESDAY — Holy Communion
6.00	THURSDAY — Holy Communion
12.30	FRIDAY — Holy Communion

Tea and coffee is available in the canteen after the main Sunday Services and visitors are most welcome.

The church is open daily.

There is an excellent bookshop just inside the main entrance.

TUBES: Charing Cross and Leicester Square.

For further information ring (01) 930 0089 between 10 a.m. and 6 p.m.

ST. ALBAN THE MARTYR
Brooke Street, Holborn

The church of St. Alban the Martyr, Holborn, is a hidden treasure in Brooke Street that is well worth discovering. The original church built by Butterfield in 1862 was destroyed by enemy action in 1941. After the war the parish first set about rebuilding the church school, after which a lovely new church designed by Adrian Scott was built and finally consecrated in 1961. The new St. Alban's, which is a perfect blend of 'ancient and modern', has height and light. Above the High Altar is a striking mural, painted for love by Hans Feibusch, an Austrian Jew who escaped persecution by the Nazis. He later painted the Stations of the Cross and through his art has become a Christian. The courtyard of the church welcomes you with Feibusch's statue of ''Jesus being raised from the dead''. The steeple of the old church remains.

The people of St. Alban's have always worshipped the Lord in the beauty of holiness. On Sundays the 9.30 a.m. Mass, both simple and congregational, is attended mainly by parishioners. The 11 a.m. Solemn Mass with its superb music and impeccable ceremonial attracts many people who live outside the parish. Later in the day there is a Said Mass for a smaller number of people who value a quiet intimate service. After the 11 a.m. Mass there is usually wine and coffee and on a warm summer Sunday it may be enjoyed in the small pleasant courtyard.

Each weekday there is at least one Mass, and very often two. St. Alban's is very conscious of its ministry to the people who work in the neighbouring offices and shops, and the many elderly people in the local blocks of flats. For over a hundred years it has been a stronghold of the Anglo Catholic Faith, and in its early days saintly priests like Father Machonochie and Father Stanton suffered that they might practice that faith.

More recently St. Alban's has been described as a happy church with a youthful and welcoming congregation. Add to this, fine music and good preaching and you will understand why it is worth a visit.

The neighbourhood around the church is so closely associated with Charles Dickens that the Mortuary Chapel (part of the old church) stands on the site of 'Fagin's Den'.

INFORMATION

SUNDAY SERVICES

9.30 a.m. Sung Mass

11.00 a.m. Solemn Mass

5.30 p.m. Said Mass

Visitors are welcome to stay for coffee or wine after the 11.00 a.m. Mass.
On Festivals there is usually a Parish Lunch.

WEEKDAY SERVICES

12.30 p.m. Mass: Monday to Friday

6.30 p.m. Mass: Wednesday and Friday

9.30 a.m. Mass: Saturdays and Bank Holidays

Nearest Tube: Sundays: Holborn, St. Paul's and Farringdon.
Weekdays: Chancery Lane and Farringdon.

From Holborn—walk along High Holborn and you will come to Brooke Street (on the left) shortly after crossing the Grays Inn Road.

From St. Paul's—follow Newgate Street which leads into Holborn. You will come to the large red brick offices of the Prudential Insurance Company on your right. The next turn —Brooke Street—leads to the church.

From Farringdon—leaving the station turn right; continue straight on, crossing Farringdon Road; when you can go no further you are in Brooke Street.

The Church is usually kept locked after 2 p.m., but call at the Clergy House.

For further information phone (01) 405 1831.

ST. MARYLEBONE PARISH CHURCH
Marylebone Road

St. Marylebone Parish Church has long been renowned for the excellence of its music. Sunday by Sunday at the Choral Eucharist the settings of Beethoven, Haydn, Mozart, Schubert, Stravinsky, and other classical and modern composers are impeccably rendered. On Good Friday the choir performs the "Crucifixion", composed by Stainer, dedicated to the choir of St. Marylebone and performed here every year since.

Now the crypt of the church has been developed as a Centre for Christian Healing and Counselling. A medical surgery is on the site with a doctor working alongside the priest, one co-operating with the other in the care of the whole person—a new partnership between religion and medicine. The offices of some of the churches' healing organisations have made their home here. The Churches' Council for Health and Healing, the Guild of St. Raphael and the Institute of Religion and Medicine are among them.

The present church was built in 1817—the fourth parish church of this ancient parish. Dedicated to St. Mary, it was originally St. Mary by the Tyburn (river) which was eventually abbreviated to St. Mary Burn and so St. Marylebone. The architect was Thomas Hardwick. Nash built the terraces at the entrance to Regent's Park opposite a few years later, to produce the magnificent complex of buildings at the York Gate.

Many famous names are associated with the parish. Charles Wesley was buried in the churchyard of the old church at the top of Marylebone High Street. Nelson's daughter by Lady Hamilton was baptised Horatia at the font. Charles Dickens lived next door and wrote several of his novels there. Robert Browning and Elizabeth Barrett were married in the 'new' church in 1846.

Today this magnificent city church looks to the future as it becomes a place of pilgrimage for the sick, of counselling for the distressed, and of grace to all who need God's help. On the first Sunday evening of each month a healing service is held when the congregation is often two hundred or more.

INFORMATION

SUNDAY SERVICES

8.00 a.m.	Holy Communion
11.00 a.m.	Choral Eucharist
6.30 p.m.	Evensong (except first Sunday: Ministry of Healing)

Coffee is available after the main Sunday services and the excellent church bookshop is open.

WEEKDAY SERVICES

1.10 p.m.	Wednesday — Holy Communion
6.00 p.m.	Thursday — Holy Communion

TUBES: Baker Street and Regents Park.

The church is opposite York Gate and almost opposite Madame Tussaud's; it is normally open in the morning.

For further information phone (01) 935 7315 during office hours.

HOLY TRINITY CHURCH
Brompton Road

Holy Trinity Church is somewhat hidden by the large Brompton Oratory. However if you walk up a short avenue situated between the Oratory and Brompton Square you will find one of the larger West End Churches standing in an oasis of peace away from the noise and bustle of the Brompton Road.

Built in Gothic style by T. L. Donaldson in 1829 the parish church of Brompton (now joined with the parish of St. Paul, Onslow Square) has always exercised a caring, evangelical ministry. There is a large active congregation, numerous Bible Study Groups, and a weekly lunch in support of Christian Aid. The church is also outward looking with the 'Trinity Team' leading missions in various parts of the country.

In a previous guide to London churches I wrote: 'To this church all are welcome: let no one feel a stranger here'. The same words apply today, perhaps more so, for in recent years Holy Trinity has been touched by the charismatic movement and experienced renewal. This congregation is alive and well — ready and eager to welcome visitors to London.

INFORMATION
SUNDAY SERVICES

8.00 a.m.	Holy Communion (1662 said)	every week
9.00 a.m.	Holy Communion (Series 3 sung)/breakfast	not week 1
11.00 a.m.	Morning Prayer (1662 sung)	not week 1
	Holy Communion (Series 3 sung)/lunch	week 1
	Creche provided.	
6.30 p.m.	Informal Evening Service	not week 3
	Holy Communion	week 3
	both with prayer and ministry	not week 5
	Family Service in Church or Church House	week 3

Coffee/lunch after the morning service—there is a good bookstall.

WEEKDAYS

12.30 p.m.   Wednesday — Holy Communion

12 noon   Thursday — Lunch in Church House

The church is in Brompton Road near the junction with Exhibition Road.

TUBES: Knightsbridge or South Kensington; (the church is about 400 yards from either).

For further information phone (01) 581 8255 between 9.30 a.m. and 5.30 p.m. Monday to Friday.

BLOOMSBURY CENTRAL BAPTIST CHURCH

Bloomsbury Baptist Church had quite a distinguished start to life for not only was it the first nonconformist chapel to stand prominently on a main London thoroughfare, but also was built by Sir Morton Peto, one of the great railway contractors, who built a variety of public buildings including Nelson's Column and the Houses of Parliament.

During its comparatively short history the church has been served by some faithful ministers, including Dr. Townley Lord and more recently, Dr. Howard Williams, who has served this city church for over a quarter of a century. Howard Williams soon realised that this central London church was no longer serving a local congregation. Church members were scattered over a wide area and they included a lively student body of young people living away from home. In fact the church situated at the northern end of Shaftesbury Avenue had the world on its doorstep, and he sought to make the premises more adaptable to present day needs.

In March 1962 a reconstruction scheme was launched and work began to update the Victorian interior of the chapel. Dark pews were stripped to a lighter colour, the organ resited and a gallery removed. The result was a bright modern sanctuary within the old frame.

With this completed the builders moved downstairs to transform the old basement into a comfortably furnished lounge and canteen. In 1967 the bright and cosy 'Friendship Centre' was ready for use—somewhere where people could meet and eat, enjoys a cup of coffee and have a wash and brush up.

For the past eighteen years visitors have come to Bloomsbury not only to worship, but also to join the church family for coffee, lunch, or a cup of tea. Most Sundays over a hundred stay for a cup of coffee after the morning service. Sunday lunch follows which is a real family affair with between 100 and 120 taking advantage of the facilities. Once a month there is an informal programme of music on Sunday afternoons, at other times people just relax in an easy chair, read, or have a nap. Tea is served around a quarter to five and after the evening service there is tea and biscuits.

This church, with the world on its doorstep offers worship, fellowship, and friendship to the many visitors who make their way there.

INFORMATION

SUNDAY SERVICES
11.00 a.m. & 6.30 p.m.

Coffee—lunch—afternoon tea available in the Friendship Centre Downstairs.

WEEKDAYS
Tuesdays lunch 12.30—1.15 p.m. (buffet)

Talk with Discussion 1.15—1.45 p.m.

Wednesdays 6.00 p.m. onwards, refreshments.

7.30 p.m. Talk with Discussion.

Fridays—(During Term Time)

John Clifford Society for Students and Nurses.

Meal from 5.30 p.m. (optional)

7.00 p.m. Meeting—Speaker or Bible Study.

This church is not open daily.

TUBE: Tottenham Court Road.

For further information phone (01) 836 6843.

CROWN COURT CHURCH OF SCOTLAND
Russell Street, Covent Garden

Until a few years ago Covent Garden was the home of London's principal market for flowers, fruit and vegetables. More recently the area has become part of the tourist scene with market stalls, craft shops, and restaurants attracting visitors from all over the world.

To the east of the market is Russell Street once famous for its Coffee Taverns and now bordered along one side by the famous Drury Lane Theatre. On the other side of Russell Street by the Fortune Theatre is the Crown Court Church of Scotland.

Crown Court Church goes back traditionally to a presence in Scotland Yard, Whitehall. It was there that the Scottish Commissioners used to worship and when the church was destroyed, a gathered congregation there moved to St. Martin's Lane and from thence to Covent Garden. Here, Scots have worshipped since 1719 and the present church was rebuilt in 1909. It serves an extensive Scottish community drawn from all parts of London and the Home Counties. It participates in activities in Covent Garden and reaches out to the many who seek help and strength in faith and life in the Christian Community.

INFORMATION

SUNDAY SERVICES
11.15 a.m. & 6.30 p.m.

Tea and coffee are available for visitors after the services and a modest lunch is also available after the morning service.

MID-WEEK SERVICE
is held on Thursday at 1.05 p.m. followed by coffee.

TUBE: Covent Garden.
Alternative Tubes: Leicester Square and Holborn.
This church is open daily, during the summer months.
For further information phone (01) 836 5643 (Church).
(01) 278 5022 (Manse).

WESLEY'S CHAPEL
The Mother Church of World Methodism

Wesley's Chapel—the Mother Church of World Methodism (a church of some twenty-four million members) is obviously a place of pilgrimage for Methodists and well worth the short journey to City Road for anyone who is visiting London.

In 1776 John Wesley purchased a piece of land from the Corporation of the City of London in order to build an adequate Chapel for his rapidly growing number of followers in the Metropolis. He appealed for funds and by April 1777 the work of building the City Road Chapel had begun. The new Chapel was duly opened by the founder on All Saints Day, November 1st 1778.

During the nineteen seventies the chapel was completely restored and re-opened in the presence of the Queen and Prince Philip on All Saints Day 1978, just two hundred years to the day from the original opening by John Wesley.

The restoration of Wesley's Chapel was but the start of a long term restoration programme to the other buildings in the complex. Wesley's house, a characteristic eighteenth century dwelling where Wesley had spent his last years, was lovingly restored and re-opened by the Prime Minister Mrs. Margaret Thatcher on Wesley Day May 24th 1981. The restoration of the other buildings in this peaceful complex continues; they include:— The Radnor Room, The Benson Building which houses the Wesley Community, the Foundery Chapel, the Chapel Keeper's House, and the Manse.

Sunday September 2nd 1984 was yet another Red Letter Day in the History of Wesley's Chapel when crowds came to City Road for the opening of the Museum of Methodism in the restored Crypt. The Museum houses many treasures, as well as many interesting exhibits from overseas.

Wesley's Chapel—the Mother Church of World Methodism is seen at its best on Sundays when the Minister, Dr. Ronald Gibbins, welcomes visitors from all over the world who join the regular congregation for worship. During the summer months the congregation swells to anything between 250 and 400 as visitors, many of whom are friends and benefactors of Wesley's Chapel, come to City Road to worship, to renew friendships, or maybe stay to lunch and the weekly 'Wesley Walkabout', or visit the museum.

INFORMATION

SUNDAY SERVICES
11.00 a.m.

The Sunday Service with Eucharist followed by Coffee in the Radnor Hall, Lunch Programme and Wesley Walkabout.

(last Sunday in the month: Morning Prayer)

WEEKDAY SERVICES
Thursday 12.45 p.m. Mid Week Service.

The Wesley Community say the Daily Offices at 8.00 a.m. and 6.00 p.m. (in the Foundery Chapel) with Eucharist on Wednesday mornings; all are welcome.

Wesley's Chapel, Wesley's House, and The Museum of Methodism are open Monday to Saturday 10.00 a.m. — 4.00 p.m.

49 City Road—directly opposite Bunhill Fields.

TUBES: Old Street and Moorgate.

For further information phone (01) 253 2262 (office hours).

FRIENDS HOUSE

Friends House, on the South side of Euston Road (opposite Euston Station) is the headquarters of the Religious Society of Friends (Quakers) in Great Britain. It was designed by Hubert Lidbetter, and built in 1926. Its Library houses a large collection of Quaker Literature and many 17th Century manuscripts, including the Journal of George Fox.

INFORMATION

Sunday Meeting 11.00 a.m.

TUBE: Euston.

Alternative Tubes: Kings Cross, Euston Square.

The Friends Book Centre (Bookshop of the Society of Friends) is open Monday to Friday 9.30 a.m.—5.30 p.m.

For further information phone (01) 387 3601.

The Westminster Friends Meeting House is at 52 St. Martin's Lane, London W.C.2.

Sunday Meeting 11.00 a.m. (with children's class)

Weekday Meetings Tuesdays and Thursdays 1.00—1.30 p.m. Wednesdays 6.15—7.00 p.m.

Tubes: Charing Cross, Leicester Square.

For further information phone (01) 836 7204.

Meetings at the above time are *open to all*.

WESTMINSTER CATHEDRAL
Ashley Place, Victoria

Westminster Cathedral, in the heart of London, is the Mother Church of the Diocese of Westminster. It stands on a piece of land once used by the Benedictine monks (who built Westminster Abbey) as a market and fair ground. After the eviction of the monks at the Reformation the site was used successively as a maze, a pleasure garden, and a ring for bull-baiting. In 1826 a prison was built there and the strong foundations which remained proved to be a great asset when Cardinal Manning bought the site in 1884 to build a Catholic Cathedral.

The foundations of the new Cathedral were completed in 1896 and in 1903, just seven years later, this large Cathedral—built in the early Christian Byzantine style—was in use for public worship. Some twelve and a half million hand made bricks were used in the construction and the building blends well with the neighbouring Victorian buildings. The 273 ft. high campanile is part of the London skyline. The tower (accessible only by lift) is open during the summer months, offering a wide panoramic view of Central London from the four balconies.

In 1976 re-development of its Victoria Street property by the Church Commissioners of the Church of England provided a pedestrian piazza in front of the main entrance. The Cathedral can therefore now be seen in its full architectural significance.

The interior with the High Altar, Crucifix and Cathedra is very impressive. The spacious nave can seat over 1,000 people, and either side of the nave are chapels, rich in marble and illustrative mosaic. The Blessed Sacrament Chapel on the far left (set aside for private prayer) and the Lady Chapel on the far right, are particularly striking.

Westminster Cathedral is served by a College of Chaplains, and a resident Boys' Choir. The "Voice of the Cathedral" also includes lay clerks, organists and Master of Music, all contributing to celebrations worthy of this House of Prayer and

Worship. Here day by day people come to receive the Body of Christ at the Eucharist, and then go out to share His love in the world.

This is perhaps best illustrated by "THE PASSAGE", a Day Centre for the Homeless opened in 1980 and run by Westminster Cathedral and the Sisters of Charity of St. Vincent de Paul as a joint response to the growing problem of homelessness in the area. Here the Cathedral offers food, warmth, friendship, advice and medical care—concrete expressions of God's love—to those most in need.

INFORMATION

SERVICES

Sunday	Masses	7.00, 8.00, 9.00 a.m.
		10.30 a.m. (Solemn sung)
		12.00, 5.30, 7.00 p.m.
	Prayer	10.00 a.m.
		3.30 p.m.
Mon.-Fri.	Masses	7.00, 8.00, 8.30, 9.00, 10.30 a.m.
		12.30, 1.05 p.m.
		5.30 p.m. (Solemn sung)
	Prayer	7.40 a.m.
		5.00 p.m. (Check with notices)
Saturday	Masses	7.00, 8.00, 8.30, 9.00 a.m.
		10.30 a.m. (Solemn sung)
		12.30 p.m.
		6.00 p.m. (First Mass of Sunday)
	Prayer	7.40 a.m.
		5.30 p.m.

The Cathedral is open every day, normally from 7.00 a.m. to 8.00 p.m.

There is a **Gift Shop** inside the Cathedral and a **Bookshop** outside.

The nearest Tube is VICTORIA.

Walk along Victoria Street and you will see the Cathedral on your right.

THE CITY TEMPLE
Holborn Viaduct

The City Temple is the main central London Church of the United Reformed Church (brought about by a union of Congregationalists and English Presbyterians in 1972 and now joined by the Churches of Christ).It has a reputation for good preaching and lively worship—its Sunday morning worship at 11.00 a.m. is fairly traditional and its evening service at 6.30 p.m. is informal and participatory with a group of musicians and occasional drama.

Historically it is one of the oldest Free Churches in London having links with a fellowship dating from the 1570's. Its first minister at the official founding in 1640 was Dr. Thomas Goodwin, Oliver Cromwell's chaplain.

The fellowship has always met within the City of London and settled at its present site in 1875, where the famous Victorian preacher Dr. Joseph Parker ministered to large crowds. Between 1936 and 1970 there were often queues to get into services led by Dr. Leslie Weatherhead, well known for his broadcasts and his work in Christian psychology.

During the second world war all but the front wall was destroyed by enemy action and the congregation worshipped in a number of churches around London, returning to a new building opened by the Queen Mother in 1958. The Queen Mother returned in 1983 to celebrate the Silver Jubilee of the new church.

The current membership of about 175 is obviously smaller than it was but it includes a strong core of very committed young people. There are many activities, and house groups meet in a number of houses around London. Great emphasis is put upon evangelistic outreach.

As well as the Sunday services there are lunchtime meetings on Tuesday, Wednesday and Thursday and visitors to this famous centre of preaching are always welcome.

INFORMATION

SUNDAY SERVICES

11.00 a.m. & 6.30 p.m.

Coffee and tea available and lunch is available on the first Sunday of the month.

The church has a good bookstall.

WEEKDAY SERVICES

Tuesday and Wednesday lunchtime meetings 1.15 — 1.45 p.m.

Thursday 1.15 p.m. Service with address
(Coffee and sandwiches available)

The small chapel is open daily—
viewing of the church by appointment.

NEAREST TUBE: St. Paul's.

For further information phone (01) 583 5532.

The City Temple is in Holborn Viaduct near Holborn Circus.

Printed by Chester Printers Limited, Chapel Lane, Corby, Northants. Telephone: Corby 2327.